THE GUIDE TO
WOODEN
POWER
BOATS

THE GUIDE TO
WOODEN
POWER BOATS

Photographs by Benjamin Mendlowitz
Text by Maynard Bray

W.W. Norton & Company
New York • London

Other books of photography by Benjamin Mendlowitz:
Wood, Water & Light
A Passage in Time
The Book of Wooden Boats
The Guide to Wooden Boats

Design by Sherry Streeter, Brooklin, Maine
Production by NOAH Publications, Brooklin, Maine

Printed by Tien Wah Press, Singapore
First edition

Library of Congress Cataloging-in-Publication Data
   The guide to wooden power boats / photographs by Benjamin
Mendlowitz : text by Maynard Bray.
           p.   cm.
   Includes index.
   ISBN 0-393-04660-5
   1. Motor Boats 2. Wooden boats. 3. Yachts 4. Photography of boats. I.
Bray, Maynard. II. Title

VM341.M46 1998
623.8'231--DC21

W.W. Norton & Company, Inc., 500 Fifth Avenue, New York, N.Y. 10110
W.W. Norton & Company Ltd. 10 Coptic Street, London WC1A 1PU
http:web.wwnorton.com

1 2 3 4 5 6 7 8 9 0

*T**his book is dedicated to our wives,*
Deborah and Anne, without whose
support the book couldn't possibly exist.
We also wish to thank designer Sherry
Streeter, editor James Mairs, and
Stephen and Maureen Corkery, Claire
Cramer, Julie Mattes, and Jeryl Schreiver
who all worked with us on this book.
Our appreciation extends to the count-
less boat designers, boatbuilders, boat
owners, and sailors through whose
efforts these beautiful craft are created,
restored, and maintained.

Contents

Foreword

One of the pleasures of having friends like Benjamin Mendlowitz and Maynard Bray is that once in a while they ask me for help with one of their projects. *The Guide to Wooden Power Boats* is the second book of this type that the authors have brought us. They have conspired to photograph, title, and outline a comprehensive and delightful guide, right down to Maynard's own "sound effects" for the engines dear to his heart.

The first *Guide to Wooden Boats* just bowled me over. Where else could you find a collection of every type of wooden sailboat you have ever wished to sail? Well, I think that this second book covering powerboats holds every bit as much downright beauty as its predecessor. The chapters cover a wide variety of each type of boat, each shown in its native setting. If variety is truly the spice of life this book proves it. Just as wood, fastenings, and machinery combine to make these vessels, the irresistible forces of Benjamin's photographs and Maynard's words—or, more appropriately, their art and prose—make for a miniature masterpiece in this volume.

I have always been pretty dreamy about boats. I've owned a lot of them—both power and sail—and have crewed on even more, and no boat has ever escaped my dreaming of how much fun it would be to take her out. This book inspires such dreams in spades. Magically, I'm at sea—voyaging over the horizon to a new harbor, an anchorage up under a beach, or the cove just around that headland for tonight's chowder.

One advantage to photographing powerboats is their mobility in lack of wind. To the photographer looking for that memorable shot there is no need for a "spanking breeze." Flat water with its reflections and spray patterns can make the picture as dramatic as if taken in a gale-force wind.

Joel White did a lot of writing to accompany Benjamin's work, including the foreword to the first volume in this series. His words are on the mark and not to be improved upon: "[Benjamin's] photography is invariably appealing, for the boat is always shown from the most favorable angle; the lighting is strong or even dramatic, and the background attractive without being intrusive.... [Maynard] strives to convey the boat's personality with his brief captions.... [His] knowledge of wooden boats is...encyclopaedic, inquisitive, and admiring." These gifts certainly are every bit as evident in this effort. Having both these books on your cabin shelf or at home all winter will give you beauty for the eye, reference for the mind, and, above all, wonderful dreams for the future.

Stephen L. Corkery
Shelter Island, New York

Launches

Aida II   25'11" x 5'6" • Designed and built by Fay & Bowen Engine Co. • Geneva, New York • 1915

As with many nautical terms, the word launch may mean different things. We use the following definition: A launch is (usually) a small powerboat having little or no cabin that goes slowly *through* instead of rapidly *over* the water. *Aida II*, pictured opposite, is representative. She's powered by a gasoline engine, although electric motors, steam engines, and diesels also furnish power for launches. In this chapter, you'll find launches of many ages and configurations with a variety of power plants. Launch hulls may be built with either transom sterns or as double-enders, like *Aida II*. Generally, launches are daytime boats without sleeping accommodations. They tend to be smooth-water boats and operate on freshwater lakes, rivers, and streams. Because speed isn't normally a launch's virtue, there is no great demand nowadays for this type of boat. But a hundred years ago, when the first gasoline engines became available, a launch became the boat of choice for many.

Before gasoline engines were perfected, steam prevailed. But steam, for all its merits, wasn't the right type of power for a "people's boat." A license was required to operate a boiler, and fuel (wood or coal) presented handling problems that were beyond most amateurs. Occasionally steam boilers exploded. In short, a steam plant was too far from a turn-key operation.

Electricity works well in launch-type hulls. Electric launches were used extensively even before the turn of the century. Their high cost, however, has kept battery-powered electric boats from developing significance in the marketplace. One hopes that, in the future, that may change.

Naphtha-powered launches enjoyed a couple of decades of popularity while gasoline engines were being developed. The naphtha engine was self-contained and compact. Many were sold—almost always for launch use—but now they've almost vanished, most likely because the volatile fuel presents a fire hazard. We have yet to see an operating naphtha-powered launch at any of the antique boat gatherings we've attended.

Grand Laker

20'0" x 3'6" • Designed by Kenneth Wheaton • Built by Kenneth and Chris Wheaton • Grand Lake Stream, Maine • 1992

MORE THAN JUST A CANOE whose stern has been cut off for an outboard motor, these Grand Lake boats are purpose-built by the professional guides who use them. Compared to conventional wood-and-canvas canoes, Grand Lakers are more burdensome and carry their width farther aft, to provide support for an outboard motor. They'll quickly scoot you out to where the fish are with only a 7½-horsepower motor.

Electricity

24'6" x 4'1" • Designed and built by Salters of Oxford • England • 1921

SILENCE ADDS TO THE ENJOYMENT of pastoral scenes, and it was this realization that resulted in the development of electrically powered canoes for day trips on England's River Thames. Facing forward, you can focus totally on the beauty of the passing landscape without the distraction of having to paddle or listen to the noise of an internal combustion engine.

Baisong

18'6 x 4'8" • Designed and built by Dispro Boat Co., Ltd. • Port Carling, Ontario, Canada • 1920

CLOSELY RELATED TO THE OAR-PROPELLED ST. LAWRENCE SKIFF, dispros (an abbreviation for the many boats built by the Disappearing Propeller Boat Company between 1915 and 1925) allow beaching without fear of underwater damage. The propeller, its shaft, and skeg can be easily retracted into a cavity built within the hull, after which you're ready for a picnic ashore. In this mode, the boat becomes, in effect, a simple rowboat.

Virginia

23'0" x 4'5" • Designed and built by Natale Riva • Torriggia, Italy • 1925

VARNISHED HULLS LAST BETTER IN FRESH WATER than in the harsher ocean environment, and if the boat is small it can be sheltered ashore where it's out of the weather and free of the water except when in use. Stored this way, a wooden boat's life expectancy is vastly extended, and the day-to-day maintenance cut way down.

Candide

27'3" x 5'8" beavertail launch • Designed and built by James Taylor & Bates • Chertsey, Surrey, England • ca.1920

RESTORED TO ITS ORIGINAL ELEGANCE, *Candide,* trailered from her native England for an antique boat rendezvous, is a perfect match for the natural beauty of northern Italy's Lake Como. Here, the modest speed of a displacement launch allows leisurely appreciation of what's all around.

Kittiwake

40'0" x 7'0" • Designed and built by T.W. Hayton • Windermere, Cumbria, England • 1898

WOOD-FIRED STEAM LAUNCHES ARE STILL A COMMON SIGHT on Lake Windermere in England's Lake District, thanks to the steamboat museum located there. The museum keeps its fleet operating during the summer season, and offers scheduled rides—always in near silence—in its steamers. It is like turning back the clock an entire century.

Sultan

24'0" x 6'0" • Rebuilt by Peter Freebody & Co. • Hurley, Berkshire, England • 1978

BUILT FOR NEITHER ROUGH SEAS NOR OPEN WATER, low-sided steam launches are very much at home running slowly past the bucolic shoreline of the upper Thames. Here, *Sultan* is near Peter Freebody's shop, where she and similar river craft are brought to be properly restored.

Walter & Edgar

30'0" x 7'0" • Built about 1895 and restored from derelict by Gary Weisenburger • Oakdale, Connecticut • 1984

ROUND STERNS HARMONIZE WELL with the smooth operation of a steam engine. The taller the smokestack, the better the draft and the more efficiently the fuel (in this case coal) will burn—just like your fireplace at home. A tall stack also keeps the smoke well away from the passengers.

Lightning

28'0" x 5'0" • Designed by Bert Hawker • Built by Greavette Boats, Ltd. • Gravenhurst, Ontario, Canada • 1946

LAUNCHES CAME IN ALL MANNER OF HULL SHAPES upon the arrival of gasoline engines a century ago. Because speed was not paramount, designers and builders were able to focus more on utility and styling. Double-ended launches found favor and were sometimes designed to give the *appearance* of speed by means of rakish stern profiles like *Lightning*'s.

Boondoggle

26'0" x 8'0" • Designed and built by Gidley • Penetanguishene, Ontario, Canada • 1914

LESS SPORTY LOOKING THAN *LIGHTNING,* but every bit as useful, this double-ender is operated from the stern by means of a side-mounted steering wheel. Without the protection of a canopy, wide-brimmed straw hats are standard garb in the warmth of the Florida sunshine.

Duchess

22'0" x 5'0" • Designed and built by Fay & Bowen Engine Co. • Geneva, New York • 1915

FLAGS ALWAYS IMPROVE A BOAT'S APPEARANCE, and, as an addition to the outfit of a launch with little else showing above the height of the deck, flags are considered a must. Bench seats, such as these in *Duchess*, photographed on Lake George, New York, became popular for boats as well as "horseless carriages" of the era.

Paddy

25'11" x 5'0" Torpedo model • Designed and built by Fay & Bowen Engine Co. • Geneva, New York • 1905

COAMINGS OF STEAM-BENT OAK NOT ONLY LOOK GOOD, BUT ARE OFTEN EASIEST TO BUILD—provided, of course, you have sufficient clear, straight-grained wood and proficiency at making it flexible through steaming. Flexibility requires an hour of steaming per inch of thickness, after which the wood will wrap tightly enough to fit into the curved space outlining *Paddy*'s cockpit.

Cocktail Betty

24'0" x 5'0" junior runabout • Designed and built by Fay & Bowen Engine Co. • Geneva, New York • 1926

SOMETIMES CALLED AUTOBOATS because their arrangement of engine, steering wheel, and seating matched that of a car, early launches also boasted equivalent ease of operation. But there were subtle differences, such as the need to navigate clear of shallow water and mind the weather, which can quickly change even on serene Lake Placid. And, of course, there's the lack of a brake pedal.

Blythewood III

37'0" x 7'6" • Built by Ditchburn Boats Ltd. • Gravenhurst, Ontario, Canada • 1927

GLASS-WINDOWED SHELTERS ALSO WERE POPULAR, as were forward cockpits. Passengers who sought a wind-in-the-hair ride and didn't mind occasionally getting wet with spray chose to sit in the open, forward of the engine. The more sedate enjoyed the ride from behind glass, near the helmsman—a good place to be on this blustery day on Lake Muskoka.

Panther

30'0" x 6'5" • Designed and built by Gibbs • Teddington, Middlesex, England • 1934

SOME LAUNCHES WERE CONVERTIBLES, with canvas canopies supported by oak, ash, or steel bows. Details such as gilded striping and scrollwork and perfectly aligned fastenings in the topside planking bespeak the care taken to build, restore, and maintain such craft. *Panther* shares the same home waters as *Panorama* on the facing page.

Panorama

25'0" x 5'4" slipper stern launch • Designed and built by Peter Freebody & Co. • Hurley, Berkshire, England • 1989

WATERBORNE ELEGANCE ON THE RIVER THAMES often comes from Peter Freebody's shop in Hurley, where new life is worked into discarded and weather-beaten relics by craftsmen who have the know-how and owners who have the funding. Having turned out rivercraft for many generations, the Freebodys know what is appropriate even when refurbishing an incomplete relic or building a new boat like *Panorama* to an old style.

Lady Genevieve

40'0" x 7'0" beavertail saloon launch • Designed and built by James Taylor & Bates • Chertsey, Surrey, England • ca. 1928

SHELTER SEEMS TO BE A PRIORITY in this double-ender. She has a permanent, windowed cabin aft for shelter from England's frequent rain, and an awning over the forward cockpit for shelter from the sun on good days.

Lady Hamilton

29'4" x 6'9" • Designed and built in England • 1929

OFFERING PATINA AS WELL AS PRIVACY, this gasoline-powered launch belongs, oddly enough, to the Lake Windermere Steamboat Museum where, of course, most of the boats are steamers. Patina—a mellowing of a surface through age or use—shows here mostly as dark spots over the heads of plank fastenings; it imparts a unique character to be cherished that's simply not achievable in newly built craft.

Mervin E. Roberts

26'1" x 7'3" converted Monomoy surfboat • Designed and built by U.S. Coast Guard • ca. 1930

SURFBOATS AND LIFEBOATS MAKE PRACTICAL CONVERSIONS, being ruggedly built and exceptionally seaworthy. They adapt readily for either sail or power, and, barring major alterations, remain recognizable. Although surplus boats of this type with wooden hulls invariably sell at bargain prices, they are getting more difficult to locate now that most such craft are being constructed of metal or fiberglass.

Goslin

20'0" x 5'6" • Designed and built by Cape Cod Shipbuilding Co. • Wareham, Massachusetts • 1927

A WATERBORNE EQUIVALENT TO THE MODEL T, power dories were among the most affordable of all the early powerboats because they were so easily built. Their Massachusetts builders had only to enlarge their commercial rowing dories, add a deck, and provide an enclosed compartment for the engine in the stern to diminish some of the noise and smell.

Handy Billy

18'0" x 5'0" • Designed by Harry Bryan • Built by Bryan Boatbuilding • St. George, New Brunswick, Canada • 1997

DESIGNED FOR SEAKINDLINESS along the lines of one of William Hand's V-bottomed boats, and laid out for quiet running with its four-stroke outboard inside a sound-dampening engine box, this newly built craft is unique. Pushed along by only 15 horsepower, fuel economy is another of her virtues.

Harmony

22'0" x 6'8" • Designed by Charles Gomes • Built by Richard S. Pulsifer • Brunswick, Maine • 1992

ONE OF THE VERY BEST WOODEN LAUNCHES STILL BEING PRODUCED is the Pulsifer Hampton with its strip-planked hull and inboard diesel engine, shown here off Mt. Desert Island, Maine. More than 60 have been built to date, all of them sold before they were completed. The canvas spray hood provides shelter when needed, but it can be unsnapped and removed when the weather is fair.

Philip Law

22'0" x 7'0" St. Pierre dory • Designed and built by The Rockport Apprenticeshop • Rockport, Maine • 1989

TIPPINESS IS THE DORY'S CHIEF SHORTCOMING, but, if you stay seated in the middle, there are few small boats that can match it for seaworthiness. With high ends and flaring sides, this hull shape rides the waves like a duck without fear of swamping, although, as with any boat caught out in rough seas, you must slow down and give her time to rise to oncoming waves.

Polly

18'0" x 4'10" lakes launch • Built in upstate New York • 1896

THE HARMONY BETWEEN A ROUND STERN AND AN OVAL, STEAM-BENT COAMING SHOWS CLEARLY HERE, along with the beauty of varnished wood. This is the archetypal open launch—about as pretty a shape as you'll find. Having the steering wheel ahead of instead of behind the engine box takes some getting used to, but it provides more space for the operator.

Merlin

25'2" x 7'3" • Probably modeled and built by Hinton Electric Co. • Victoria, B.C., Canada • 1904

STILL IN EVERYDAY USE as the means of getting to and from an island home near Sidney, B.C., *Merlin* puts many miles under her keel in the span of a year. Until recently, an old, slow-turning, three-cylinder Vivian gasoline engine provided the power, giving off a comforting *puk-a-ta, puk-a-ta, puk-a-ta* sound well matched to this venerable double-ender. A somewhat more recent Graymarine powers her now.

Little Bear

22'6" x 7'6" • Designed by Murray G. Peterson • Built by Norman H. Hodgdon, Jr. • Boothbay Harbor, Maine • 1965

ENHANCED BY THE LOW MORNING LIGHT against a dark sky, *Little Bear* holds up well to scrutiny no matter what environment she's in. It's apparent that the designer and builder understood one another in their execution of this charming yet useful launch.

Runabouts & Raceboats

Foxy Lady
19'0" x 6'0" barrelback runabout • Designed and built by Chris-Craft Corp. • Algonac, Michigan • 1939

I f you're looking for a fast boat, this is the chapter for you. Most of these boats can manage 25 mph and several will do an easy 50 miles an hour or more. The dividing line between a fast launch and a slow runabout is hazy, but generally, the boats you'll see in this chapter are planing boats that rise when you advance the throttle to skim over the water at 20 miles per hour or more. To plane, a boat requires a flattish bottom beginning amidships and running all the way to the stern. It also must be reasonably light in weight compared to its power; even the smallest runabout requires an engine of at least 15 or 20 horsepower. Once planing, the more power you give a boat, the faster it goes—provided the water stays calm. When waves ruffle the surface, the shape of a planing boat's bottom greatly affects whether or not it can keep up its calm-water speed. A V-shaped bottom that splits the oncoming waves and throws them aside is a must in the forward part of almost any powerboat.

Runabouts appeared a century ago and evolved right along with the automobile. The early fast launches were first known as "autoboats." Styling as well as technology came, to some degree, from the automobile. When cars were given sloping windshields, boats followed. Likewise tail fins, chromed fittings, convertible tops, and dashboards—there are many parallels.

Varnished mahogany topsides and decks gave runabouts an elegant look and were the choice of most manufacturers. This treatment worked well for a freshwater environment, while for saltwater use, boats tended to be custom-built and more plainly finished.

Pure raceboats require more powerful engines, generally smaller cockpits with less seating, and are far more costly than runabouts. We include boats that range from a 35-mile-an-hour Gold Cup winner of 1908 to an up-to-date, three-point hydroplane designed for speeds up to 180 miles an hour.

Olive

24'0" x 7'0" fast outboard boat • Designed by R.D. (Pete) Culler • Built by Hadden & Stevens • Small Point, Maine • 1995

DESIGNER PETE CULLER'S SIGNATURE IS ALL OVER THIS BOAT, from the sculpted stemhead with intersecting forward rails cut out for bow chocks to the Chesapeake-style, cross-planked V-bottom. *Olive* gets up on a plane easily with a 70-horse outboard, and handles well wide open, even in choppy water.

Gramp

25'0" x 5'10" • Designed by William H. Hand, Jr. • Built by L. West and George Bonnell • Port Chester, New York • 1915

***GRAMP*'S DESIGNER LED THE FIELD** in creating fast and seaworthy V-bottomed launches and runabouts in the decade before World War I. The rough waters of Buzzards Bay served as Hand's proving ground, and his plans, once drawn, were offered, along with instructions and the required special fittings, to potential owners who saved money by building their own boats. Hundreds of "Hand V-bottoms" were so built.

Abaco

19'5" x 6'10" • Designed and built by Albury Bros. • Man-o-War, Abaco, Bahamas • 1984

YOU CAN ALWAYS COUNT ON HULL SHAPES THAT EVOLVE FROM HARD USE. Few have been more thoroughly tested than the Albury runabouts built in Man-o-War in the Bahamas. They're steady, heavy, and surprisingly dry when pushed through rough water. So appealing was her performance that Benjamin Mendlowitz brought *Abaco* to Maine, making much of the trip by water, to use as his own photo boat.

Bevie C.

23'0" x 8'4" • Designed by Ernest MacKenzie • Built by MacKenzie Cuttyhunk • Hyannis, Massachusetts • 1971

ANOTHER BOAT RESPECTED FOR ITS ROUGH SEA ABILITY is the bass boat developed by Ernest MacKenzie. With an inboard engine for power—and for the quick maneuvering necessary when fishing among rocky shores where the bass hang out—you can steer by tiller rather than wheel. Besides the conventional tiller aft, there's another at the forward end of the cockpit, along with duplicate engine controls.

Raven

28'0" x 7'6" • Designed and built by Chester Clements • Southwest Harbor, Maine • 1932

THERE'S A LOAD OF ROOM IN *RAVEN'S* BIG COCKPIT for the wide variety of tasks she's put to, and a melon-type canvas spray hood at the ready (shown here furled along the forward port side deck) should the wind breeze up and passengers want shelter from the spray. Because of their similar shapes, the spray hood fits the coaming perfectly, raised or lowered.

Meadows

30'3" x 8'0" • Built by Arno Day • Brooklin, Maine • 1955

HERE IS A BOAT SIMILAR TO *RAVEN,* both having been built along the lines of a Maine lobsterboat, but somewhat narrower. It's a toss-up whether to call them runabouts or launches. When opened up, they're quite fast, making them more of a runabout, but at idle or part throttle and when used for enjoying the scenery, the term launch applies best. No matter what label you choose, these are a pair of most useful boats.

Special K

25'0" x 7'4" Sportsman • Designed and built by Chris-Craft Corp. • Algonac, Michigan • 1941

CHRIS-CRAFT LED ALL OTHER BUILDERS of production-line wooden boats by a wide margin from the 1920s to the 1960s, and there are probably more surviving Chris-Crafts today than there are boats of all the other manufacturers combined. Each year brought new offerings—110 different models the year this boat came out.

Happiness Is... III

22'7" x 7'5" Sea Skiff • Designed and built by Chris-Craft Corp. • Salisbury, Maryland • 1955

CHRIS-CRAFT INTRODUCED ITS SEA SKIFFS IN 1954 after acquiring a new facility for building them in Salisbury, Maryland. Most notable is their lapstrake planking, which tends to soften the ride and lessen the spray. Because the laps are glued together as well as mechanically fastened, the hulls were very strong.

Elisa

29'5" x 7'2" • Built by Oscar • Venice, Italy • 1966

STILL IN USE IN HER NATIVE ITALY, *Elisa* is now based at Lake Como near the Swiss border at the base of the Alps. Originally, she served as one of the water taxis of Venice, where the streets are of water and require boats such as these and the age-old gondolas for getting about.

Wimur

26'0" x 6'0" • Designed and built by Ditchburn Boats Ltd. • Gravenhurst, Ontario, Canada • 1926

PARKED LIKE A CAR IN A GARAGE, boats on fresh water benefit from being so kept. Actually, these shorefront structures are boathouses and they're common on lakes where the water level remains constant throughout the season. Inside, there's a means of hoisting the boat clear of the water during the winter or for long periods of idleness.

Seasharp

28'0" x 6'11" • Designed and built by Chris-Craft Corp. • Algonac, Michigan • 1929

YOU MIGHT CONSIDER THIS AN UNUSUAL SETTING for a speedy runabout, but in fact it's a scene for which such a craft, because of its openness, is ideally suited. Each year, dozens of runabouts like *Seasharp* gather for a cruise southward through the waterways of northern Florida to Mt. Dora, which lies in the center of the state some 20 miles north of Orlando.

Wave

26'0" x 6'8" • Designed and built by Chris-Craft Corp. • Algonac, Michigan • 1929

ON THE ST. JOHNS RIVER CRUISE, along with her near-sister *Seasharp* and other antique runabouts, launches, and raceboats, *Wave* occasionally gets a chance to open her throttle. *Wave* is one of more than 100 standardized 26-foot runabouts built by Chris-Craft in 1929 before the Great Depression curtailed production.

Lucky Penny

24'0" x 6'2" • Designed by John L. Hacker • Built by the Hacker Boat Co. • Detroit, Michigan • 1924

PASSION PREVAILS among owners of wooden boats, and often leads to collecting and hands-on restoration. You might call it an obsessive hobby. This beautifully restored Hacker-Craft Dolphin, for example, represents but a small part of a dedicated owner's 18-boat fleet, which includes two more Dolphins.

The Golden Arrow

30'0" x 6'4" • Designed by Morris M. Whitaker • Built by Fay & Bowen Engine Co. • Geneva, New York • 1924

A STOCK MODEL "...complete in every detail, beautifully proportioned, smart, trim, and the acme of perfection. Ready for quick delivery." So claimed the builder's advertisement. We also like the fold-down windshield and, of course, the way *The Golden Arrow*, at moderate speed, splits the water so easily.

Margaret Ann

30'0" x 7'2" • Designed by John L. Hacker • Built by the Hacker Boat Co. • Silver Bay, New York • 1995

YOU CAN STILL BUY A BRAND NEW HACKER like this one—built more or less to the original plans of that gifted designer—if you place an order with Bill Morgan, a longtime Hacker aficionado, who revived the old Hacker Boat Co. in the 1980s. Morgan's new Hackers retain the outward appearance of the originals while increasing their strength to accept more horsepower.

Min

35'0" x 7'8" • Designed by John L. Hacker • Built by Coecles Harbor Marina & Boatyard, Inc. • Shelter Island, New York • 1992

ANOTHER NEW BOAT CUSTOM-BUILT TO AN OLD HACKER DESIGN is the triple-cockpit *Min*, elegantly turned out for saltwater use close to where she was built. Because of his stylish designs, interest in John L. Hacker boats has remained high and they have become favorites for replication.

Pardon Me

47'0" x 10'6" • Designed by John L. Hacker • Built by Hutchinson Boat Works • Alexandria Bay, New York • 1947

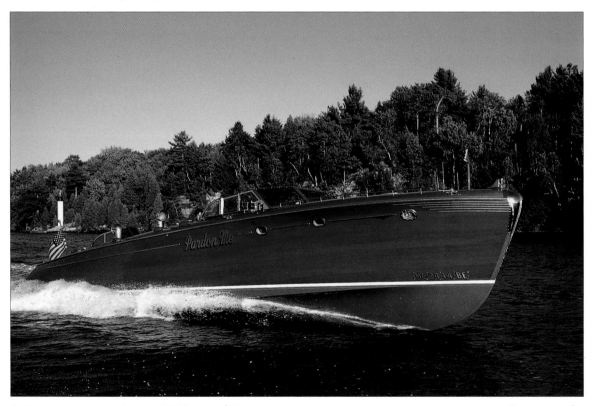

ART-DECO STYLING OF THE 1930S AND '40S APPEARED IN POWERBOATS AS STREAMLINING. Gone was the classic pre-Depression look in which vertical lines (as well as horizontal ones) played a part of each design, and in their place were rounded teardrop shapes such as the chromed bow fitting shown here. In this respect, boat styling and automobile styling ran parallel courses.

Of Course

28'8" x 8'6" Super Aquarama • Designed and built by Cantieri Riva • Sarnico, Italy • 1969

A FERRARI WOULD BE THE AUTOMOTIVE EQUIVALENT. Rivas are known for their high cost, but also for their quality and performance. The layout in *Of Course* is distinctive, with an upholstered sprawl space that extends from side to side right over the top of the engine box. Although most commonly seen on the Mediterranean, Lake Tahoe is home port for *Of Course* and several other Riva runabouts.

Comet

36'0" x 7'0" • Designed and built by Fellows & Stewart • Wilmington, California • 1921

SOME MOTORBOATS CAME FROM THE WEST COAST, although the vast majority were built near the Great Lakes and farther east. *Comet* still operates in her home state of California, serving her Lake Tahoe owners, the Owens family, as a means of basic transportation and high-end pleasure. In Tahoe, she has plenty of beautiful company.

Torpedo Too

17'0" x 6'0" Fairliner Torpedo runabout • Designed by Dair Long • Built by Western Boat Co. • Tacoma, Washington • 1948

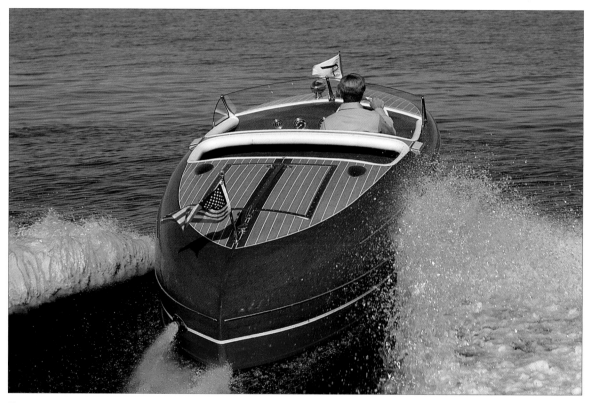

BEFORE THE TAIL FINS OF THE LATE 1950S came this neat little pointed-stern runabout, streamlined to match her name. Upon entering the annual Victoria, British Columbia, Classic Boat Festival, *Torpedo Too* came away with top honors in her class, to no one's surprise. Although offered as a stock design from 1947 to 1952, it is surprising that only 32 were ever built.

Fleetwood

26'0" x 6'0" • Designed by H.C. Minett • Built by Minett-Shields, Ltd. • Bracebridge, Ontario, Canada • 1929

THE NOISE AND WAKE ARE PART OF THE FUN, according to their owners, but that opinion is not universal. It is generally agreed, however, that varnished mahogany runabouts such as *Fleetwood* are among the most beautiful watercraft afloat.

Dix

21'0" x 5'6" • Built by Ditchburn Boats Ltd. • Gravenhurst, Ontario, Canada • 1927

BY NO MEANS ANOTHER LOOK-ALIKE, this shiny, black runabout is a kind of miniature raceboat in which the driver sits all the way aft. *Dix* also has a small forward cockpit, however, and a distinctive metal rail that runs the length of the deck ahead of the windshield.

Dixie II

39'3" x 5'9" raceboat • Designed by Clinton H. Crane • Built by Geo. F. Lawley & Son • S. Boston, Massachusetts • 1908

WHEN BRAND-NEW, THE LONG AND SKINNY RACER *DIXIE II* WON powerboating's two most coveted prizes—the Harmsworth Trophy and the Gold Cup—powered at the time by a breakthrough V-8 engine designed by Henry M. Crane, brother to *Dixie*'s designer Clinton. Exhaust pipes, then as now, projected vertically from the engine compartment.

Something Else

28'0" x 9'0" unlimited hydroplane • Designed by C. Douglas Van Patten • Built by Bill Morgan • Silver Bay, New York • 1982

AFTER 80 YEARS OF EVOLUTION, raceboat speeds have risen from *Dixie II*'s 35 miles an hour to an anticipated 180 for this three-point hydroplane—a design in which air resistance becomes as important as the drag caused by the water over which she skims.

Miss Florida

19'0" x 6'2" Race Boat • Designed and built by Chris-Craft Corp. • Algonac, Michigan • 1937

CHRIS-CRAFT BUILT MORE THAN 50 BOATS LIKE *MISS FLORIDA* over the course of three years beginning in 1935. With thinner planking, more powerful engines, and distinctively painted topsides instead of the usual varnish, they were assigned the special Chris-Craft designation of Race Boat. The Chris-Craft archives, now preserved at The Mariners' Museum in Newport News, Virginia, are a wonderful resource for owners and historians.

Scotty-Too

26'0" x 6'6" Gold Cup raceboat • Designed by John L. Hacker • Built by the Hacker Boat Co. • Mt. Clemens, Michigan • 1929

AVERAGING ONLY ABOUT 50 MILES AN HOUR, *Scotty-Too*, shown here on Lake George, came in second to *Hotsy Totsy* in the 1930 Gold Cup Race. The raceboats that year were to run a distance of 90 miles in a single day (3 heats of 30 miles each) on the Navesink River near Red Bank, New Jersey. Seven started, but due to breakdowns of potentially faster boats, only three made it to the third heat.

Baby Bootlegger

29'10" x 5'11" • Designed by George F. Crouch • Built by Henry B. Nevins, Inc. • City Island, New York • 1924

COMPARED TO THE SINGLE-PURPOSE HYDROPLANES that followed her, this winner of the 1924 and 1925 Gold Cup—a raceboat's most prestigious trophy—makes a fine gentleman's runabout when there's no race to be won. She's smooth riding and well mannered even at 60 miles an hour, and for striking good looks she is incomparable.

Miss Columbia

26'10" x 6'3" • Designed by George F. Crouch • Construction coordinated by Mark Mason • New England • 1986

THE DESIGN IS A CONTEMPORARY OF *BABY BOOTLEGGER* on the facing page, but it is less radical in above-water appearance. The original *Miss Columbia* was also a Gold Cup raceboat and also designed by George Crouch. Although the original didn't survive, her plans did, allowing this faithful replica to be built some 60 years later.

Power Cruisers

Power Cruisers at Mystic Seaport   Mystic, Connecticut

Power cruisers are boats fitted for sleeping and cooking and short vacations away from home. Their speeds vary, and a few with big engines can climb up on top of the water and plane like the boats in the preceding chapter. Most, however, are of the semi-displacement type, meaning that they're capable of 12 to 18 miles an hour, but fuel economy suffers above a 9 or 10 mile-an-hour cruising speed.

Powerboating is noisier than sailing and in general represents less of a challenge to seamanship. Sailors sometimes scoff at powerboaters, but any kind of boating can be fun—that's what pleasure boating is all about. Every type of boat has its list of advantages and drawbacks, and if you're aware what these are, you can use your boat in such a way as to maximize its strong points and minimize its weaknesses.

Power cruisers, or cabin cruisers as they're sometimes called, are usually skippered by their owners. Many are family boats, built in wood primarily between 1920 and 1960. As the type developed, these boats became wider and higher. Both one-of-a-kind custom boats and standardized boats that came off a production line are featured in this chapter.

When a boat is big enough to cruise in, routine maintenance becomes a serious issue. No boat here is beyond what a single person can maintain provided he or she anticipates the boat's needs and deals with them in good time—instead of waiting until a small task turns into a major project. Timeliness in annual painting and varnishing, ensuring that there is adequate below-deck ventilation, and taking care that the hull never remains out of the water so long that the planking dries and the seams open are three keys to reducing maintenance. Some power cruisers have twin engines and propellers while others are of the single screw type. Engines are either gasoline (quieter, cheaper, and not as smelly) or diesel (safer and more reliable).

Daisy

29'0" x 9'0" • Designed and built by Norton Bros. • Newport, Rhode Island • 1929

A RAISED FOREDECK MEANS FULL HEADROOM, even in a boat as short as *Daisy*. Cooking, eating, and sleeping take place under this deck, leaving the varnished deckhouse to function primarily as a shelter for the helmsman. Because it has no back, the deckhouse becomes part of the cockpit and provides a windbreak for those who gather there to enjoy the warmth of a sunny day.

Rozzy

42'0" x 10'0" • Designed and built by Dawn Boat Co. • Clason Point, New York • 1927

WITHOUT A SKYLIGHT IN HER FOREDECK, *Rozzy*'s cabin beneath would be very dark since the round ports cut into the side of the hull don't admit much natural light. Those opening ports, however, can admit fresh air at times when the skylight and foredeck hatch have to be closed due to rain.

Gezira

55'0" x 12'6" • Built by Taylor's • Chertsey, Surrey, England • 1932

HEAVY WEATHER WON'T TROUBLE THIS BOAT'S CREW since most of the operating and living are carried on inside. Those venturing outside to raise the anchor or launch the tender, on a blustery day such as this in Scotland, do so with the added security of lifelines that run from bow to stern.

Tuva

32'0" x 9'3" • Designed and built by Gray Boats • Thomaston, Maine • 1929

ONLY A LITTLE RAIN CAME from the retreating squall, but *Tuva*'s crew was taking no chances. They buttoned on the side curtains just in case. Now that it's clearing, they'll head for shore. Boarding the peapod tender astern is made easier by the ladder—a necessary piece of gear for any boat with this much freeboard.

Mer-Na

36'0" x 9'0" Blanchard 36 • Designed by Leigh Coolidge • Built by N.J. Blanchard Boat Co. • Seattle, Washington • 1931

POWER CRUISERS OF THE PACIFIC NORTHWEST TEND TO HAVE LARGE CABINS and small cockpits because of the damp climate. Spectacular views, such as the southern end of Saltspring Island, are also among this coast's features, so you want lots of windows in the deckhouse.

Danae

40'0" x 9'0" • Designed by L.E. Geary • Built by Vancouver Shipyards • Vancouver, B.C., Canada • 1930

***DANAE* STEERS FROM THE FORWARD DECKHOUSE,** which has been raised for better all-around visibility—and to provide enough space beneath for the engine. *Danae*, like *Mer-Na*, carries an easily launched dinghy for scouting the Pacific Northwest's many interesting shores.

Scamper

36'0" x 9'0" • Designed and built by C.W. Harris • Seattle, Washington • 1920

YOU'RE *IN* A BOAT LIKE THIS, NOT *ON* IT. You even step down from the deck when you enter the pilothouse. The result is a low profile that gives *Scamper* a big-boat appearance. Her interior is roomier than expected, thanks to a high-crowned cabin top and cabin sides that run all the way to the rails.

Rhinegold

36'0" x 8'6" • Designed and built by Vancouver Shipyards • Vancouver, B.C., Canada • 1910

DOUBLE-ENDED POWERBOATS LIKE THIS WENT OUT OF STYLE after engines became more powerful without taking up any more space. With lighter engines, displacement cruisers could speed along at 12 or 15 knots instead of 7 or 8—provided their sterns were wide enough to keep them from squatting at these speeds. *Rhinegold*'s slippery hull, at the slower speeds, still has the edge, however, when it comes to fuel economy.

Isabel

38'0" x 11'0" • Designed and built by the Matthews Co. • Port Clinton, Ohio • 1926

STEERING FROM THE COCKPIT LETS YOU PARTICIPATE in the conversation when passengers gather there. You'd call *Isabel*'s a family-style layout, and it's altogether different from earlier days when yachts were operated by professional sailors kept at separate stations, remote from the owner and his party.

Patrician

38'10" x 11'0" Matthews 38 • Designed and built by the Matthews Co. • Port Clinton, Ohio • 1941

ALTHOUGH BUILT DURING THE ERA OF AGGRESSIVE STREAMLINING, *Patrician,* true to her name, appears stately with her conservative styling. Little wonder the Matthews 38s became such popular standardized cruisers.

Summertime

49'0" x 13'0" • Designed by Chris Nelson • Built by Dawn Boat Co. • Clason Point, New York • 1941

AFTER A THOROUGH REBUILD, *SUMMERTIME* LOOKS BRAND-NEW. Even her sheer received attention, shown here restored to its proper line. She returns each fall to Rockport Marine in Maine, the yard that did the restoration work, so that she can be maintained by those who have come to understand her best.

Duchess

39'6" x 12'3" • Built by Sound Marine Construction Co. • Greenport, New York • 1950

THE SERENE CURVE OF AN UNBROKEN SHEER—high forward and low aft—gives *Duchess* much of her distinctive appearance. Although her superstructure is busy because of its various levels and window sizes, the deckhouses do not dominate or confuse the eye, both because of the strong sheer and the uniform finish. That finish is varnish—much maligned due to the need for regular care, yet incomparably lovely.

Brayton Point

40'9" x 12'1" Sportsman 40 • Designed and built by Huckins Yacht Corp. • Jacksonville, Florida • 1959

ADVERTIZED AS HAVING "QUADRACONIC" HULLS, the Huckins power cruisers' snappy performance was due as much to light construction as to this modified V-bottom shape. Being built with two layers of diagonally laid planking gave Huckins yachts a skin of additional strength and made possible the elimination of some conventional heavy framing.

Maaken II

44'6" x 11'10" • Designed and built by The Elco Works • Bayonne, New Jersey • 1940

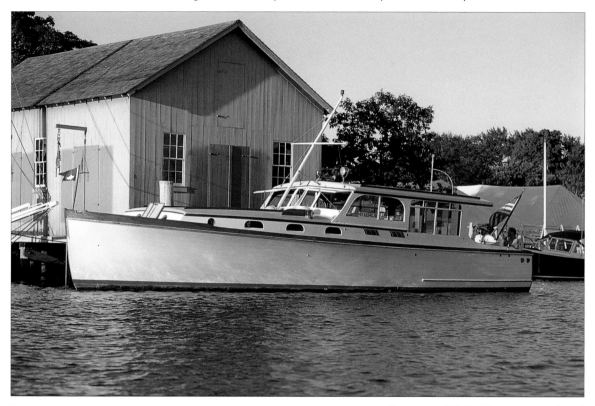

BOATS WITH THIS SORT OF LAYOUT BECAME KNOWN AS SEDAN CRUISERS because of their likeness to enclosed automobiles. Here, the top of the trunk cabin is the equivalent of the hood of an automobile and the driver steers just aft of the windshield near where the passengers normally ride.

Copper Star

38'0" x 10'0" • Designed and built by Chris-Craft Corp. • Algonac, Michigan • 1929

ONE OF THE MOST USEFUL OF ALL THE OFFERINGS of this prolific builder, these 38-footers were especially handsome because of their low profile. The reward for enduring open-air steering and cockpits without awnings was a racy-looking boat. Inside the cabin were the galley, the accommodations for seating and sleeping, an enclosed head, and direct access to that wonderful forward cockpit.

Foto

33'0" x 8'10" • Designed by F.K. Lord • Built by Kanno Boat Builders, Inc. • City Island, New York • 1929

THE WORKHORSE OF MARINE PHOTOGRAPHER MORRIS ROSENFELD, *Foto* was for many years a familiar sight in Long Island Sound and waters farther east, chasing sailing yachts as they spread their wings to race or cruise. Those exciting days were far behind, however, when Edmund Cutts discovered her, run down and in desperate need of help. He gave this once-familiar craft new life through a complete restoration.

Pot O' Gold

42'0" x 11'0" • Designed by Paine, Belknap & Skene • Built by Geo. F. Lawley & Son • Neponset, Massachusetts • 1930

IF YOU'RE GOING TO INVEST IN AN EXPENSIVE RESTORATION, the boat you choose makes a difference. A yacht's pedigree carries as much weight as a dog's, except here the "parents" are the designer and builder. This boat surely measures up as a blue blood, and, throughout her life, has received better care because of it.

Jericho

42'0" x 11'8" • Designed by Raymond Bunker • Built by Bunker & Ellis • Manset, Maine • 1957

A SINGLE SHOP TURNED OUT THE MOST APPROPRIATE BOATS for the wealthy summer residents of Mount Desert Island and other nearby Down East resorts. Until the partners grew too old to continue building their classics, known simply as Bunker & Ellises, they never lacked for new orders.

Kittiwake II

44'0" x 13'0" • Designed by Raymond Bunker • Built by Bunker & Ellis • Manset, Maine • 1964

UNLIKE *JERICHO* ON THE PRECEDING PAGE, this Bunker & Ellis has always had more paint than varnish and has but a single engine. While twin-screw boats, with their duplicate power plants and controls, enjoy a reputation for reliability and maneuverability, many seasoned sailors prefer the steadiness of a single, centerline propeller that's deep in the water and free from cavitation even when the boat rolls in a beam sea.

Caribou

38'6" x 10'6" • Designed by Leroy Wallace • Built by Newbert & Wallace • Thomaston, Maine • 1952

POWER CRUISERS BASED ON MAINE LOBSTERBOATS ENSURE A SEAKINDLINESS often missing from standardized designs. There's generally more of the boat under the water and less above, giving an easier and more stable ride in rough water. A steadying sail helps dampen the roll when the wind is abeam, and the boom also serves to hoist the pram onto the afterdeck.

Sea Scribe

38'0" x 12'0" • Designed by Carroll Lowell • Built by Even Keel Boatshop • Yarmouth, Maine • 1985

VISIBILITY IMPROVES DRAMATICALLY when you ascend to the flying bridge atop the cabin. Equipped with a second steering wheel and duplicate engine controls and instruments, this becomes the helmsman's favored location in fair weather.

Boss Lady

43'0" x 12'6" • Designed by Eldredge-McInnis • Built by Rockport Marine • Rockport, Maine • 1978

FOR CRUISING CONVENIENCE, an anchor that can be easily dropped and retrieved is paramount. For power-boats, a short bowsprit or anchoring platform with a sheave in its outer end does the job. But the anchor and chain still have to be washed free of mud while being brought aboard, and having rails to hang on to while standing on the narrow perch eliminates much of the hazard.

Day Boat

28'0" x 8'6" • Designed and built by Frank L. Day, Jr. • Brooklin, Maine • 1970

BUILDER-OWNED, this simple cruiser looks at first like a lobsterboat. Little wonder, since lobsterboats are a specialty of the shop. It's an old-time kind of place where boats are moved in wooden cradles on a sloping skidway. A simple rope lashing secures the boat to its cradle for moving.

Charlena

31'0" x 8'0" • Designed and built by Newell McLain • Thomaston, Maine • 1943

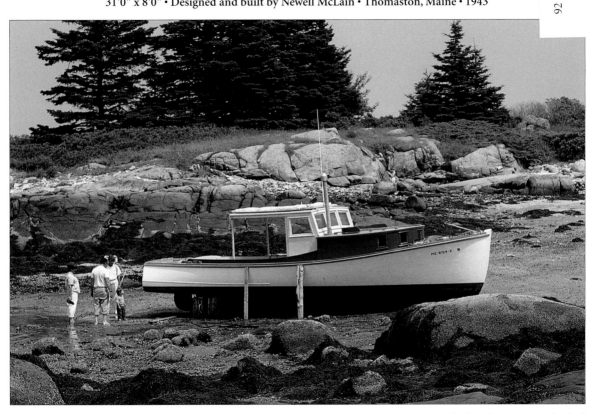

BOATS ARE GROUNDED OUT FOR A VARIETY OF REASONS, including painting and clearing a rope-fouled propeller. The latter situation provoked this grounding. The firm beach keeps the keel from burrowing and provides a good base to work from.

Kintore

36'10" x 11'0" • Designed by Wm. Garden & Jas. Mitchell • Built by The Artisans College & Malone Boatbuilding • Rockport, ME • 1995

FLOPPER STOPPERS PREVENT MOST OF THE ROLLING that plagues powerboats. They consist of a metal paravane or "fish" hung from an outrigger on each side of the boat so it can "swim" underwater. So rigged, the paravanes (because they aim downward when the boat moves ahead) keep enough tension on the outriggers to resist rolling.

Paquet V

42'0" x 11'6" • Designed by Henry A. Scheel • Built by Geo. I. Hodgdon, Jr. • East Boothbay, Maine • 1982

THIS SMALL SAIL IS STRATEGICALLY LOCATED aft of amidships to help keep *Paquet* head-to-wind when at anchor. Ranging back and forth with the wind first on one side then the other, as many powerboats do when moored or anchored, is not only annoying, but in a crowded anchorage risks collision with other boats. Aboard *Paquet*, however, there'll be no such concern.

R&R

55'0" x 16'0" • Designed by Roy Merritt • Built by Merritt Boat & Engine Works • Pompano Beach, Florida • 1981

ROUGH WATER AND BOATS LIKE *R&R* WERE MEANT FOR EACH OTHER. Just to see this sportfisherman in action, we set her up to run through our wake. With hulls designed to maintain speed in rough water and bring fish aboard in the cockpit at the stern, these boats also offer tasteful luxury inside the cabin.

Tintinajo

36'0" x 12'0" • Designed and built by Rybovich & Sons Boat Works • West Palm Beach, Florida • 1959

HEADING EAST THROUGH AN INLET near West Palm Beach and into the Gulf Stream, *Tintinajo* will soon be stalking Florida's various sport fish—dolphin, wahoo, kingfish, and the hard-fighting but elusive sailfish. It's often a rough ride to and from the fishing grounds but these special-purpose boats easily handle the challenge. Once near the fish, maneuverability enhances the chances of hooking the quest.

Motoryachts & Motorsailers

Mohican
65'0" x 12'0" • Designed and built by Consolidated Shipbuilding Corp. • Morris Heights, New York • 1929

Most of the boats in this chapter are true yachts in the traditional sense. They're big, and usually are managed day-to-day by paid professionals who also operate them unless an owner chooses to take the helm. Marinas and private docks are where most are berthed; you won't often find them lying to anchors, except when cruising. These craft carry their tenders and dinghies on board instead of towing them. Rarely, if ever, do they have identical sister vessels; they're almost always custom-designed and custom-built. You'll find few that aren't impeccably maintained, with their varnish gleaming and their brass shining from daily polishing.

The smaller, faster motoryachts that once carried their owners back and forth to work are called commuters. Although these days that kind of use is rare, commuters still retain their appeal because they are among the sleekest of all watercraft. *Mohican,* shown on the facing page, falls into the commuter category even though she no longer commutes.

Motorsailers conclude this chapter. Generally, they are craft of exceptional seaworthiness, and speed is secondary. The sails not only serve to back up the engine should it fail, but they also steady the boat from rolling too deeply in a beam sea. This adds greatly to the onboard comfort. Most motorsailers have enclosed steering stations that eliminate having to "suit up" and "brave the elements" when it rains. If you're planning a long voyage at sea and want to make it in comfort, by all means consider a motorsailer.

Principia

96'0" x 18'6" • Designed by L.E. Geary • Built by Lake Union Drydock • Seattle, Washington • 1928

HER STATELY PROPORTIONS AND CLASSIC DETAILING took root far back in history, and, by understanding this early aesthetic, designers like Ted Geary created beautiful vessels like *Principia* and *Canim* (on the facing page). *Principia*'s substance and rugged beauty inspired Philadelphia's Independence Seaport Museum to select her for refurbishing as a charter vessel.

Canim

96'0" x 19'0" • Designed by L.E. Geary • Built by Lake Union Drydock • Seattle, Washington • 1930

BUILT A BIT FANCIER THAN HER NEAR-SISTER *Principia*, *Canim* still appears substantial. Because such yachts built on the West Coast had hulls of old-growth Douglas fir, they survived longer than their oak-framed, iron-fastened East Coast counterparts.

Columbia

111'4" x 20'0" • Designed and built by Mathis Yacht Building Co. • Camden, New Jersey • 1931

FULL-WIDTH CANOPY DECKS BENEFIT THE WOODWORK as well as the passengers situated beneath them. The varnish on *Columbia*'s teak cabin sides lasts longer with less exposure to direct sunlight, and the people who gather near the stern are protected from sun or rain. In fact, the aft deck, when buttoned in with curtains, remains perfectly usable even in bad weather. *Columbia* (ex-*Captiva*) now carries the name *Commodore*.

Tiger

93'0" x 18'0" • Designed by James McCallum • Built by Munroe's Shipbuilding • Oban, Scotland • 1927

MOTORYACHTS USE STEEL DAVITS to lower and retrieve their tenders—davits that swing inboard so their load can be placed in chocks on deck. Aboard *Tiger*, all is ready for the tender's return: Fenders are in place, and the boarding platform (supported by its own davit) is rigged. The tender hoists easily thanks to the electric winches mounted on the boat davits.

Radiant

110'0" x 18'0" converted subchaser • Designed by Sparkman & Stephens • Built in Newport, California • 1943

A SECOND STEERING STATION atop the pilothouse increases the helmsman's visibility dramatically and is the place to be on such a fine day. Even when motoring through a crowded anchorage in darkness—or avoiding errant logs or coming alongside a dock—this would be the helmsman's favored location, and he is helped by the powerful searchlights mounted nearby.

Yellowfin

107'1" (registered length) x 26'10" converted freight and supply boat • Designed by H.C. Hanson • Built 1943

MANY VESSELS BUILT FOR WARTIME DUTY were of unusual strength and durability, yet relatively few conversions like *Yellowfin* have survived. Robust rather than elegant, such surplus vessels built of the very finest materials once sold at bargain prices.

Black Knight

82'7" x 19'9" • Designed by Eldredge-McInnis, Inc. • Built by Goudy & Stevens, Inc. • East Boothbay, Maine • 1968

HER NAME MANDATES THE APPROPRIATE COLOR, but black topsides require more attention than light colors because the planks soak up so much more of the sun's heat that they're prone to drying and shrinking. Black paint tends to blister if there's even a trace of moisture under it, so a good painter always assures himself of a dry surface before he begins. *Black Knight*'s flawless topsides exemplify the good care she's given.

Yorel

83'0" x 20'0" • Designed by Eldredge-McInnis, Inc. • Built by Hodgdon Bros., Inc. • East Boothbay, Maine • 1989

BOATBUILDING SKILLS HAVE LONG BEEN ASSOCIATED WITH THE EAST BOOTHBAY COMMUNITY, as *Black Knight* and *Yorel* demonstrate. They're basically of the same design, but more than two decades separate their launchings.

Portola

81'0" x 19'6" • Designed by D.M. Callis • Built by Harbor Boat Building • Los Angeles, California • 1929

OWNED AND MAINTAINED BY THE SAME FAMILY FOR OVER 40 YEARS, *Portola* has never needed restoring. She's kept in good condition by continuous, intelligent care by folks who have come to understand her best. They also operate her without the help of paid professionals—a most unusual claim for a yacht of this size.

Jessica

75'6" x 13'0" • Designed by John H. Wells • Built by Consolidated Shipbuilding Corp. • Morris Heights, New York • 1930

ANOTHER YACHT TO BENEFIT FROM LONG-TERM MANAGEMENT and care is *Jessica,* a commuter-style yacht whose professional skipper, Raymond Thombs, has been with her for more than a half century. He began in 1947 and since then has been continuously employed by a succession of owners who recognized his value.

Speedalong

55'1" x 10'6" • Designed and built by Consolidated Shipbuilding Corp. • Morris Heights, New York • 1928

CONSOLIDATED SHIPBUILDING LED ALL OTHER BUILDERS in constructing motoryachts and commuters in the years before the Great Depression. The company's success came partly from its strategic location at the northern tip of Manhattan, but mostly from the quality of its workmanship and the appeal of its designs.

Rum Runner II

58'0" x 12'0" • Designed and built by The Elco Works • Bayonne, New Jersey • 1929

A FITTING NAME FOR SUCH A FAST AND SLINKY CRAFT—one which was typical of the mysterious fleet that sought to outsmart and, if caught, outrun the Coast Guard during the 11 exciting years of Prohibition, which ended in 1933.

Liberty

79'10" x 15'0" • Designed by Bruce King • Built by Hodgdon Bros., Inc. • East Boothbay, Maine • 1996

BEDECKED WITH FLAGS, *LIBERTY* **AWAITS** the coming tide and the final roll of the trailer wheels into the water. Launching day is a time of great celebration, representing as it does the completion of months of dedicated effort by the builders. It's also a test of the designer's talents, and the first of many rewarding days for the owner, who will use her for touring the Maine coast in style and at speeds up to 38 mph.

Aphrodite

74'0" x 14'6" • Designed and built by Purdy Boat Co. • Port Washington, New York • 1937

AS COMMUTERS, IT FELL TO FAST AND SLEEK YACHTS like *Aphrodite* to transport their owners between their Long Island or Hudson River estates and their New York City offices. Beyond convenience, part of the fun came from racing other commuters. Such rivalry led to purpose-built flyers like this one with top speeds in excess of 40 mph. *Aphrodite* inspired the creation of *Liberty* on the facing page.

Ragtime

64'0" x 12'6" • Designed and built by Consolidated Shipbuilding Corp. • Morris Heights, New York • 1928

TYPICALLY, COMMUTERS LOOKED LIKE THIS—always fast, but also sufficiently large and capable of making weekend runs to Newport and other summer resorts with safety and reliability. The years 1928 and '29 brought waterborne commuting to its zenith; the numbers dwindled thereafter during the Depression.

Kiyi

50'0" x 10'4" • Designed by Leigh Coolidge • Built by Schertzer Bros. • Seattle, Washington • 1926

PROPORTIONS PLAY AN IMPORTANT ROLE in producing a handsome yacht, and in a yacht of such exquisite proportions as *Kiyi* one could overlook her small size and imagine her at twice her actual length. So distinctive and lovely is she to look at, however, that you're not at all disappointed to learn of your mistake.

Thunderbird

55'0" x 11'10" • Designed and built by John L. Hacker • Bay City, Michigan • 1940

OF THE COMMUTER STYLE, *Thunderbird* was created for use on Lake Tahoe, and that spectacular body of water is still her home. She's clearly from the streamlined era—a time when automobiles and locomotives as well as boats took on aircraft characteristics. All were meant to look fast, and some, like the 70-mph *Thunderbird*, really were.

Bingo

60'0" x 18'0" sportfisherman • Designed by Andy Mortenson • Built by Norseman • Miami, Florida • 1964

HOPE TOWN IN THE BAHAMAS IS HER HOME PORT. Navigating in those sometimes shallow but transparent waters works best at times by "reading" the bottom. A brown color, instead of the usual aquamarine, indicates shoal water. Spotting from *Bingo*'s flying bridge makes for easier reading, as you're able to see shoal water far ahead.

Tonda

67'7" x 15'9" • Designed by Frederick C. Geiger • Built by John H. Trumpy & Sons • Annapolis, Maryland • 1960

KEPT IMMACULATE IN ALL RESPECTS, this motoryacht's flaring bow and gilded scrollwork mark her as a Trumpy. (That's the letter "T" that begins the scroll—backwards on starboard, correct on port.) While some motoryachts frequently drop anchor, it is a rare occurrence for others. *Tonda* appears to be in the latter group, but she nevertheless carries a davit to help get the anchor aboard without scraping those perfect topsides.

Cassiar

64'0" x 14'9" • Designed by B.T. Dobson • Built by Palmer Scott • New Bedford, Massachusetts • 1949

TWIN SCREWS MAKE A BOAT MORE MANEUVERABLE, and, if you know how, you can steer with the engines alone. *Cassiar*'s rudders were entirely out of commission during this photo session, yet she remained under complete control throughout, by the skillful adjustment of her port and starboard throttles.

Yonder

28'0" x 9'8" • Designed by John G. Alden • Built by Harvey F. Gamage • South Bristol, Maine • 1934

COMFORT, NOT SPEED, RANKS HIGH in motorsailer appeal. Five or six knots would be *Yonder*'s cruising speed under power, and she'll make another knot or so at full throttle or under sail alone in a snapping good breeze with the wind abaft the beam. But she's roomy and her motion is easy on her crew—and on board it's always interesting as there are so many combinations of sail and power to try out.

Hurricane

40'2" x 11'3" • Designed by Concordia Co. • Built by Casey Boat Building Co. • Fairhaven, Massachusetts • 1939

THIS BOAT CAN SAIL BETTER THAN MANY MOTORSAILERS because her sloop rig is larger than most. Undoubtedly, she could carry even more sail if her ballast keel were lower but that would compromise her ability to anchor in thin waters. As is, *Hurricane* requires only five feet of water depth to float—a foot less than a pure, keel-type sailboat of her size.

Condorline

45'0" x 10'0" converted steam pinnace • Built in 1909

CONVERTING A NAVAL CRAFT TO A SHORT-RIGGED MOTORSAILER results in a boat that is practical, and, if done with the good taste of this one, can really be quite attractive. Here, the sails are more for steadying than for sailing—that is, to dampen the tendency of the boat to roll when the waves come at her sideways.

Nor'Easter

59'3" x 16'2" • Designed by William H. Hand, Jr. • Built by Charles A. Anderson • Wareham, Massachusetts • 1927

LONG HAILED AS THE FIRST TRUE MOTORSAILER, this husky craft inaugurated others of similar character that soon became branded as "Hand motorsailers," taking their name from their imaginative and talented designer. They're all as able as they are good looking.

Burma

57'6" x 15'0" • Designed by R.O. Davis • Built by Henry B. Nevins, Inc. • City Island, New York • 1950

R.O. DAVIS BEGAN HIS CAREER AS A DRAFTSMAN for William Hand, during which time he drew the plans for *Nor'Easter* on the preceding page. Later, on his own, Davis's designs continued to evolve Hand-type motorsailers which culminated in the design of *Burma*—lighter and more yachtlike than her predecessors.

Hawksbill

56'0" x 15'0" • Designed by John G. Alden • Built by Hodgdon Bros., Inc. • East Boothbay, Maine • 1965

NOT MANY MOTORSAILERS HAVE CLIPPER BOWS, but *Hawksbill*'s lovely bow is one of her most distinctive features. Another characteristic—one that she shares with most all yachts of her genre—is underway shelter for the helmsman. On *Hawksbill*, even the upper steering station atop the deckhouse has been protected from the weather.

Working Boats

Miss Sylvia
53'7" x 18'5" shrimp trawler • Built by Charles Elmer Clemmons • Supply, North Carolina • 1973

When America was young, working craft dominated on all its shores. Without roads, goods traveled by water. Fishing craft numbered in the thousands. Ferries carried people sometimes great distances, and ran on published schedules. With the coming of railroads, trailer trucks, and passenger cars, and the network of roads they now run on, the need for coastal freight boats and ferries dramatically diminished. It's fishing now that keeps most wooden working craft in business. Those fishing boats, along with tugboats and ferries, make up most of the present coastal wooden working boats on the nation's waterways as well as in this chapter.

As the 20th century rolled on, people found themselves with increasing amounts of leisure time and disposable income. Pleasure boating gained ground throughout these years and the numbers of workboats diminished. Opportunities for converting working boats to pleasure boats occurred, and a few such craft are placed in this chapter simply because they have essentially retained their original workboat appearance.

Fancy finishes such as varnish and gloss paint are rare for boats that are expected to earn their owners' living because there's constant and unavoidable wear—often year-round. Paint work is a lot easier to maintain than varnish or high-gloss finishes, especially in light colors, but this is not to imply that working craft are inferior. Indeed, they have a wide appeal and lots of charm.

Alert

32'0" x 11'6" harbor tug • Designed and built by Martinolich Shipyard • San Francisco, California • 1946

MOST OF A TUGBOAT'S HULL LIES BELOW THE WATER because it requires a large propeller to exert maximum pull. *Alert*'s propeller, for example, is 40 inches in diameter. And since she has no cause ever to venture beyond San Francisco Bay's sheltered waters, her low freeboard works just fine.

Susan H

55'4" (registered length) x 16'0" tugboat • Built by Frank Prothero • Seattle, Washington • 1947

A TUG'S TOWING BITTS HAVE TO BE FORWARD OF THE RUDDER, otherwise she can't steer and pull at the same time. Aft of the bitts, the towline must be free to range from side to side without snagging, so the freeboard here is low and the rail clear of projections.

Delta

52'0" x 12'0" converted tugboat • Built by Turrel Shipyards • Victoria, B.C., Canada • 1889

CONVERTING A TUG TO A PLEASURE CRAFT often calls for stretching out the cabin to take advantage of the empty space on the afterdeck. The towing bitts and the fenders can be dispensed with, and with the bow thus exposed an anchor can be carried there, ready for use anytime there's a need.

Argonaut II

73'0" x 14'8" • Designed by Edson B. Schock • Built by W.B. Menchions • Vancouver, B.C., Canada • 1922

FOR YEARS, HER DUTY WAS TO THE CANADIAN FOREST SERVICE, but now *Argonaut II* serves as a yacht. The heavy, slow-turning Gardner diesel still provides reliable power and its deep-toned exhaust—*pubh-pubh-pubh*—is a welcome sound to those ashore as well as those lucky enough to be on board.

Geri II

33'0" x 8'6" trunk-cabin double-ender • Built in Steveston, B.C., Canada • 1955

THE NET REEL MARKS HER AS A GILL-NETTER and her small size reveals that she's an inshore boat. Gill-netting aboard *Geri II* requires only a single person because the reel is hydraulic and brings in or sets the net at the throw of a lever. Rollers at the stern through which the net passes protect it from sagging and tearing.

Rover

53'6" x 14'6" buy boat • Built in Astoria, Oregon • 1910

HAVING A BUY BOAT ON STATION near the fishing grounds allows fishermen to spend more time fishing by eliminating the need to run to the factories with their catch. Home waters for both *Rover* and *Geri II* are near the San Juan Islands of Washington, where many wooden fishing boats still operate.

Deadrise Boats

40' x 10' (typical) oyster tongers • Built near Tilghman Island, Maryland

DEADRISE BOATS, MOST OFTEN KNOWN SIMPLY AS DEADRISES, STILL INHABIT CHESAPEAKE BAY in large numbers. These two are returning after a day on the shallow-water oyster beds that are set aside specifically for harvesting oysters by scissoring with long-handled tongs—rugged work, because it's all done by hand. Each tong load has to be culled after it's brought aboard, and the rocks and undersized oysters thrown back.

Buy Boat

65' x 18' (typical) oyster buy boat • Built pre-World War II on Chesapeake Bay

AS ON THE WEST COAST, THE BUY BOATS OF CHESAPEAKE BAY ACCEPT THE DAY'S CATCH, tally it up and pay each dredger, and then deliver the load to shore for shipping. These buy boats, like the boats on the facing page, are V-bottomed with hard chines.

Vanity

20'8" x 9'6" scalloper and party boat • Designed and built by Manuel Swartz Roberts • Edgartown, Massachusetts • 1929

SHE DRAGGED FOR SCALLOPS in the winters and took passengers out sailing during the summer season, in a routine that continued for years. Each summer, *Vanity* shed her dragging gear, was freshly painted, had her big gaff rig installed, and became a true sailing catboat. Until he died a few years ago, Oscar Pease's livelihood came from this versatile craft.

Star

34'0" x 10'8" shipyard utility boat • Designed by Webster Eldridge • Built by Whitaker & Eldridge • Noank, Connecticut • 1950

NOANK, CONNECTICUT, BOATBUILDERS TURNED OUT MANY BOATS LIKE THIS, primarily for lobstering. Most, including *Star*, had wet wells, which were boxes built right into the middle part of the boat, and open to the sea through holes bored through the hull planking. The catch would thus remain in its natural element until sold. *Star* now operates as Mystic Seaport Museum's utility boat just upriver from where she was built.

Margaret E

49'6" x 15'3" gill-netter/troller • Built by Charles Nelson • Seldovia, Alaska • 1944

ALTHOUGH PRESENTLY RIGGED FOR GILL-NETTING with a loaded net reel at the stern, this combination boat can easily be converted for trolling, a hook-and-line method instead of net fishing. *Margaret E* is big and seaworthy enough to operate offshore—in contrast to the little inshore boat *Geri II*, featured earlier.

Roann

60'0" x 16'9" Eastern-rigged dragger • Designed by Albert E. Condon • Built by Newbert & Wallace • Thomaston, Maine • 1947

ROANN, LIKE *MARGARET E,* WAS DESIGNED FOR OPEN-WATER FISHING. She catches bottom fish by dragging a weighted net from her starboard side and running ahead slowly while the fish are scooped up. Representative of the many draggers like her, she's recently been added to the historic fleet at Mystic Seaport Museum.

Novelty

65'0" x 19'7" sardine carrier • Built by Southwest Boat Corp. • Southwest Harbor, Maine • 1944

THE NEED TO TRANSPORT FISH ASHORE BROUGHT ABOUT A SPECIALIZED VESSEL called a sardine carrier. The entrapped young herring concentrated within a fishboat's net are sucked out by a giant centrifugal fish pump that's driven by the carrier's main engine. The water spills back overboard and the fish drop into the carrier's hold, salted in layers to preserve them. When the hold is full, the carrier heads for the canning factory.

Jacob Pike

83'0" x 18'6" sardine carrier • Designed by Leroy Wallace • Built by Newbert & Wallace • Thomaston, Maine • 1949

CARRIERS ARE FACTORY-OWNED, but with the recent closing of one after another factory in Maine, the *Jacob Pike* became one of the last sardine carriers in service along that coast. Her slim and lovely lines make her a welcome sight underway or at rest. She is the last of six carriers launched from the same yard beginning in 1947, all built to the same half model.

Pauline

83'0" x 18'0" passenger cruiser • Designed by Leroy Wallace • Built by Newbert & Wallace • Thomaston, Maine • 1948

ONCE A SISTER SARDINE CARRIER to the *Jacob Pike* (preceding page), *Pauline* was converted to comfortably accommodate 12 passengers for coastal cruises lasting several days. She's proven as successful in her new role as in the original one, and illustrates how adaptable a good boat can be.

Grayling

64'11" x 12'6" • Designed and built by Frank L. Rice • East Boothbay, Maine • 1915

IN HER EARLY DAYS AS A FISHING VESSEL, *Grayling* carried a jib and loose-footed mainsail in addition to the mizzen. Later abandoned, a rig to match the original was reinstalled during this boat's recent conversion to a pleasure boat. In fact, she appears outwardly—varnished pilothouse and all—just as she did when new, more than 80 years ago. Benjamin River Marine of Brooklin, Maine rebuilt and converted her in 1996 and 1997.

Sabino

57'1" x 23'0" passenger steamer • Designed and built by H. Irving Adams • East Boothbay, Maine • 1908

LAUNCHED AS *TOURIST*, THIS FERRY'S FIRST RUN WAS ON MAINE'S DAMARISCOTTA RIVER. Renamed *Sabino* and given a higher cabin and sponsons for increased stability, she carried people up and down the Kennebec River; later she served the Casco Bay islands from Portland. *Sabino* now offers hour-long rides to visitors at Mystic Seaport Museum—still using her original compound steam engine and burning coal for fuel.

Patience

72'0" x 19'7" passenger ferry • Designed by Spencer Lincoln • Built by Billings Diesel & Marine • Stonington, Maine • 1982

IN SHARP CONTRAST TO MODERN FERRY CONSTRUCTION in steel, *Patience* was built traditionally of wood— one of the last ferries to be built of that material. It's always a joy to see a new vessel spring to life as she hits the water, ready to back off the cradle and give onlookers a chance to see her perform and perhaps even enjoy a short ride. ·

Three Fevers

20' x 7' (approximate dimensions) double-ender • Built near Redcar, Cleveland, England

THE GENTLY SLOPING BEACHES ALONG ENGLAND'S NORTHEAST COAST consist of sand so firmly packed that neither tractors nor boat trailers sink in and get stuck. Local craft like this are launched daily from the beach for fishing and pulled to safety behind the seawall when they're done for the day. Lapstrake planking adds strength and assures watertightness in this sometimes rough service.

Double-ender from Nice

20' x 7' (approximate dimensions) double-ender • Built near Nice, France

THESE SIMPLE, UNDECKED DOUBLE-ENDED FISHING BOATS share the same harbor in the south of France as mega-yachts many times their size. The fish caught from these small, seaworthy craft might well be on some upscale restaurant's menu, or served aboard one of the giant neighboring yachts.

Newfoundland Fishboat

20' x 7' (approximate dimensions) • Built near St. John's, Newfoundland, Canada

AN INGENIOUS FISHERMAN ADAPTS what's available to make his job easier. In this case, it appears that he's made use of two rubber-tired wheels, powered by the boat's engine, to haul back his fishing longline. Keeping his investment low by using a small and simple boat means he can keep more of the money he receives for his catch.

Mary Day Yawlboat

15'6" x 6'0" • Designed by Havilah Hawkins, Sr. • Built by Arno Day • Brooklin, Maine • 1962

HER DAY'S WORK DONE, this yawlboat is being hoisted clear of the water on the schooner *Mary Day*'s stern davits. The schooner has no engine, so when there's no wind—or in a crowded anchorage—the yawlboat provides the propulsion. Normally, she pushes from astern, but at times the little boat comes in handy pushing or pulling from the bow. She also carries passengers between the schooner and the shore.

Chris Dana

32'0" x 10'0" lobsterboat • Designed and built by Makinen Bros. • South Thomaston, Maine • 1952

LOBSTERBOATS CAN HEAD HOME EARLY in the afternoon because they've been at it since daybreak. Early mornings are best for hauling traps because there is less wind. Traps require less effort to haul these days thanks to hydraulic line handlers, which bring a trap up off the bottom quickly.

Tatiana

36'4" x 10'6" • Designed and built by Willis Beal • Beals Island, Maine • 1990

SOME LOBSTERBOATS LOOK YACHTLIKE they're so well painted and maintained. And on summer Sundays—when it's illegal to haul—they're occasionally used for family outings such as viewing a schooner race or picnicking on an island. The tub-type stern is rare nowadays, but its tradition goes back to the early Beals Island and Jonesport builders of Maine.

Islander

35'4" x 11'6" • Designed and built by Osmond Beal • Beals Island, Maine • 1975

WOODEN TRAPS, LIKE WOODEN LOBSTERBOATS, GET SCARCER EACH YEAR as lobstermen increasingly switch to traps of plastic-coated wire and boats of fiberglass. Newer materials have proven more efficient, yet some lobstermen stand by the long tradition of wood.

Red Top II

34'0" x 10'6" lobsterboat • Designed and built by Harold Gower • Beals Island, Maine • 1968

IT'S EASY TO UNDERSTAND WHY MAINE LOBSTERBOATS ARE SO REVERED; their seaworthiness and maneuverability comes from on-the-job testing. *Red Top* represents a good compromise in that she's neither overly wide nor overly high.

Nova Scotia Boats

40' x 14' (typical) lobsterboats • Designed and built by Doucette Boatbuilders, Ltd., and others • Nova Scotia, Canada • 1960-1983

EAST OF MAINE, THE STYLE OF LOBSTERBOATS CHANGES DRAMATICALLY. At Grand Manan, for instance, so-called Novi (for Nova Scotia) boats dominate. Their raised foredecks, plumb stems, and large pilothouses make them easily recognizable, even to an untrained eye. Structurally, there's a big difference as well. Much of their strength comes from a platform well-braced with hackmatack knees.

Glenda-Glenace

33'2" x 11'0" • Designed and built by Willis Beal • Beals Island, Maine • 1972

TIDES RANGING UPWARD FROM NINE FEET allow a Maine or Canadian lobsterman to ground out his boat for minor repairs or bottom painting. A noontime low, which occurs twice a month, is best, allowing midday work. Although it's perfectly possible to let the boat flop down on one of her bilges, both sides of the bottom are accessible if you can keep her fairly upright.

Jef

34'0" x 10'6" • Designed and built by Marriner Beal • Beals Island, Maine • 1958

PARTIALLY ENCLOSING A LOBSTERBOAT'S STANDING SHELTER makes cold-weather hauling a little more pleasant. *Jef*'s riding sail, used to keep the boat more or less head-to-wind, has been dropped because she's working so close to a lee shore.

Shepherdess

28'0" x 8'0" • Designed by Frank L. Day, Sr. • Built by Frank L. Day & Son • Brooklin, Maine • 1968

YOU CAN CRUISE IN THIS BOAT, even though she's rigged to haul traps. The accommodations are Spartan, however, so short cruises work best. *Shepherdess* is a boat that adds charm to any harbor, and her owner recognizes this virtue. She's moored in front of his home most of the time to enhance the view.

Glossary

aft, abaft Toward the stern of the boat.

barrelback runabout A runabout with an exceptionally crowned deck.

bass boat An inboard-powered boat of about 25 feet, developed especially for bass fishing, that is fast and maneuverable. Bass boats are usually fitted with a small trunk cabin and windshield forward, and a large cockpit aft.

beam The maximum width of the hull; or a timber in a boat's structure such as a deck beam.

beam sea Waves that come at a boat from the side. A beam sea causes the boat to roll more than directly oncoming or following waves.

bilge The space under the floorboards or cabin sole where water may collect; also, the curved, transitional area of a round-bottomed hull where the sides and bottom come together.

bitts Posts near the bow or stern used for tying the boat to a dock or mooring.

boom A near-horizontal spar projecting aft from a mast, and controlled by a rope called a sheet, to which a sail attaches; also, a spar attached to a mast near the deck and used for hoisting or lowering a load such as a small boat.

bow The forward end of a boat's hull.

bow chocks Fairleads adjacent to the stem at deck level through which rope can pass without chafing excessively.

cavitation An undesirable propeller performance caused by air that is drawn in or created at the propeller blades. A cavitating propeller, because it is biting into air instead of water, looses its thrust and races inefficiently.

chine The sharp corner in a flat or V-bottomed boat where the hull sides and bottom meet.

clipper bow A bow that is concave in profile and usually terminates with a decorative carving called a billethead. These bows are often further adorned with trail-boards that extend aft along the sheer from the billethead.

coaming The rim around a cockpit or deck opening that projects above deck level.

cockpit The sunken space from which the helmsman steers the boat and where the passengers congregate.

davits Stationary or swinging arms used for hoisting a small boat out of the water. Single davits are also used to lift other items such as anchors.

deadrise boat An inboard workboat from the Chesapeake Bay region with a bottom that is V-shaped and cross-planked.

deckhouse An enclosure, with windows, built relatively high above the deck that provides accommodation and shelter.

displacement boat A non-planing craft whose speed is limited by its waterline length and the waves it makes.

dory A simple, flat-bottomed boat with flaring sides that is planked longitudinally over wide-spaced, sawn frames.

double-ender A boat without a transom that is pointed at both bow and stern.

electric launch An open boat of slow to moderate speed powered by an electric motor driven by storage batteries.

forward Toward the bow.

gill-netter A commercial fishing boat equipped with a long net of mono-filament stored on a big, hydraulically powered reel at the stern.

hackmatack A species of softwood, also known as larch and tamarack, from which wooden knees are made. One tree usually produces only a single knee whose long arm comes from the trunk, and the short arm from the largest root.

hydroplane A very fast boat whose bottom is stepped to reduce its resistance when planing.

keel The major portion of a boat's backbone structure that lies between the stem and stern.

knee A grown timber or lamination with two

relatively short arms that run roughly at right angles to each other. Knees are used for connecting and/or bracing two structural members such as a frame and a deck beam.

lakes launch An open powerboat for use on freshwater lakes.

lapstrake A type of hull planking in which the planks overlap each other like the clapboards of a house.

launch Generally, a small, engine-driven displacement boat that has little or no cabin. (*See* chapter introduction, page 9.)

lee shore A coastline that is downwind from a boat.

motorsailer A boat fitted with both sail and engine that can utilize either or both for motive power. (*See* chapter introduction, page 97.)

motoryacht An engine-driven boat large enough to require and accommodate a professional captain and crew. (*See* chapter introduction, page 97.)

outboard A boat propelled by an outboard motor; also, the motor itself; also, a

direction or location toward one side of the boat from the middle.

outrigger A boom or pole that runs athwartships instead of fore-and-aft.

paravane A device that is towed underwater from the ends of outriggers (one on each side) to dampen a boat's roll. A paravane consists of a flat plate with a vertical vane along its centerline to which a cable can be shackled. Under tow, the paravane angles slightly downward and keeps a significant strain on the towline.

plane To travel fast upon the surface of the water. In order to "climb up" on top of the bow wave it creates and begin planing, a boat must have a lot of power for its weight and a hull bottom that is relatively straight in its aft portion when viewed from the side.

plumb stem A stem that is vertical or nearly so in profile.

power cruiser An engine-driven boat with cruising accommodations that is usually owner-operated and no more than 60 feet in length. (*See* chapter introduction, page 67.)

raceboat A fast, engine-driven boat created primarily to compete for speed against similar boats on a racecourse. (*See* chapter introduction, page 37.)

runabout A fast, open powerboat that planes. (*See* chapter introduction, page 37.)

semi-displacement boat A craft with moderate power whose maximum speed lies in the transition between non-planing and fully planing.

sheer The line formed by the hull sides meeting the deck; in an undecked craft, the top edge of the hull sides.

single screw An inboard powerboat with a single engine and propeller.

skeg The underwater vertical portion of the hull near the stern to which the rudder is often attached.

skiff A flat-bottomed rowboat.

spar A tapered pole, such as a mast, boom, or outrigger.

sponsons Watertight pods on each side of a boat's hull that increase stability.

stem The center, upright, forward-most piece of wood on a boat, to which the forward ends of the planks are fastened.

stern The aft, or back, end of a boat's hull.

strip planking Hull planking made of narrow, parallel strips that are edge-fastened and usually glued together.

transom The transverse portion of a boat's hull at its aft end.

trunk cabin A low cabin that projects from the deck to increase headroom within the hull.

twin screw An inboard powerboat with side-by-side engines, shafts, and propellers.

V-bottom A type of underbody characterized by a bottom that is V-shaped when viewed from bow or stern and which has a knuckle called a chine where the bottom meets the sides.

working boat A boat engaged in commercial activity such as fishing or carrying passengers for hire. (*See* chapter introduction, page 125.)

Index

About the Photographer and Author

Benjamin Mendlowitz has devoted his professional life to capturing the magic of wooden boats in color photography. His annual *Calendar of Wooden Boats* has won awards for photography, design, and printing. His work has regularly appeared in feature articles and on the covers of the most respected magazines in the boating field, as well as in many general interest magazines and books. A one-man show of his photographs has been exhibited at maritime museums around the country since it opened at the Philadelphia Maritime (now Independence Seaport) Museum. Previous books of his color photographs of wooden boats include *Wood, Water & Light*; *A Passage in Time*; *The Book of Wooden Boats*; and *The Guide to Wooden Boats*. He lives in Brooklin, Maine.

Maynard Bray has been building, restoring, and writing about boats most of his life. After 13 years as a marine engineer he became shipyard supervisor at Mystic Seaport where he directed the restoration and enlargement of the museum's watercraft collection, the construction of the shipyard, and the refloating of the whaleship *Charles W. Morgan*. In 1975 he moved to Brooklin, in his native state of Maine, and in 1979 became *WoodenBoat* magazine's technical editor. Still a contributing editor and Brooklin resident, he continues to supervise the restoration of fine wooden yachts and to write prolifically about boats in books and articles. His books include *Mystic Seaport Watercraft*, *Herreshoff of Bristol* (as co-author), and *Boat Plans at Mystic Seaport*. He has provided the text for the *Calendar of Wooden Boats* for 17 years.